the notion of family

the notion of family

BY ELEANOR MALLET

ORANGE FRAZER PRESS
Wilmington, Ohio, USA
1999

Additional copies of *The Notion of Family*, or other Orange Frazer Press publications may be ordered directly from:

Orange Frazer Press, Inc.
Box 214
37¹/₂ West Main Street
Wilmington, Ohio 45177
Telephone 1.800.852.9332 for price and shipping information

Web Site: www.orangefrazer.com;
E-mail address: editor@orangefrazer.com

Library of Congress Cataloging-in-Publication Data

Mallet, Eleanor, 1943-
       The notion of family / by Eleanor Mallet.
            p.   cm.
       Columns originally published in The Plain dealer from
       1991 to 1998.
         ISBN 1-882203-57-7
         1. Mallet, Eleanor, 1943-   --Family. 2. Journalists--United
       States--Family relatonships. 3. Mallet family.   I. Title.
         PN4874.M4763A25 1999
         070' .92--dc21
         [B]   99-32222
                                                                      CIP

To David, Louis, Max, Jon—The richness of my life.

These columns appeared in *The Plain Dealer* from
1991 to 1998. I want to express my gratitude to the
newspaper for allowing me to free rein to tell my stories.

~

Thanks to all those who had a hand each week in
readying my columns for publications: Christine Jindra,
Margaret Bernstein, Betsey O'Connell, Michael Bennett,
Fran Stewart, Fran Henry, Ellie Rhyner, Donna Hayes,
the copy editors and especially my writing friend
Karen Long. Thanks to my husband David Bergholz, who
read and reacted to each one.

~

I am indebted to Mark Schwartz and Michelle Moehler
for the design of my collection of columns,
Family Stories. Thanks also to photographers
Robert Huntsinger, Lynn Johnson, Mark Perrott;
others known and unknown; and most of all to David,
our family chronicler.

~

Cover design by J Porter
Formatting by John Hawley

contents

i n t r o d u c t i o n

The Notion of Family is a collection of stories about my family. They are selected from over 400 columns I wrote over six years for *The Plain Dealer* in Cleveland.

I wrote about many subjects; women's struggles, the public debate about family, political and local issues. I also wrote regularly about my family.

These columns — my personal stories — evoked a powerful response from many readers.

They were written of the moment, as column writing is, and in the pressure of newspaper deadline. They were also written in a random order, drawn from events as they were occurring in my life in those years.

In *The Notion of Family*, the stories are arranged chronologically. What emerges is something new — the arc of family over four generations.

The stories go deep into the intimacy of family, my relationship with my husband, sons, parents and in-laws. They are drawn from the over-filled clutter of the day, the gritty milieu of dishes, kitchen cleanser and different ideas about tidiness. Some are about the humor, strife and poignancy in the minutiae of family life. Others are about puzzling through new stages as they envelop us. Still others focus on the big life events that linger a long time, such as a parent's death.

These stories were written at a time when children were leaving home and all our parents were gone except my father-in-law, who was increasingly frail. At one level, these stories are about what to make of the losses that come with getting older, both the deaths that occur and the diminishing intimacy with children as they grow up and move away.

Looking at these essays now, what comes through to me is how interwoven are intimacy and loss. And how, as much as we go forth from family, we also reach back.

My stories are not about an ideal family or a broken one. They are about a real family, caring for and struggling with one another. They elucidate the emotional heat of these relationships, the commitment they take over a lifetime.

The stories are juxtaposed with family photographs, a different kind of record of the past. Together, I believe, they make a powerful statement about the perplexities and richness of the relationships we all live in. ❧

Eleanor Mallet

the notion of family

f a t h e r ' s   d a y

I COME INTO FATHER'S DAY EMPTY-HANDED AND HAVE FOR NEARLY ALL OF MY ADULT LIFE.

My father died of a heart attack one night at home after dinner. It was one week after his 53rd birthday. I was 23. Such are the dry facts.

Of course my life went on. But a part of me will be forever at that moment. That moment of frantically trying to call an ambulance. And a part of me will always feel abruptly severed and left — left to figure out the complicated and contradictory puzzle he was to me.

It's more than 20 years since he died. It saddens me to think how out of date he would be today. So I find myself periodically having these conversations. He would have loved to have known of the fall of communism. He would have loved to have known my husband and sons. Why, at the time he died, there was not even an ambulance equipped with oxygen, let alone modern clot-dissolving drugs that might have saved his life. And the women's movement had barely begun.

A few years ago I met an elderly man who lived in the neighborhood where I grew up. After we chatted about this and that, we discovered a connection. "I knew your parents in high school," he exclaimed. "I remember them holding hands in the halls."

That's a piece of family lore. My parents were "sweethearts" from the age of 16. I looked at this warm and wizened man and felt the enormity of the chasm death has made. My father never grew old. In my mind's eye my father was still a stocky, young man, his smooth-skinned bald head giving him a distinctive, formidable look.

Into this love match were born three girls, me in the middle. My mother's life, and therefore ours, revolved around him. Their romance became ours. My sisters and I would eat a rowdy dinner. My father arrived home later and we would gather round while she served him.

After dinner he would try to relax and read the newspaper in the living room. We would get into these frenzies, enacting elaborate plays, tumbling feats or musical recitals, squealing for his attention.

As we got older, we would put on music and get him to teach us to dance. We would follow his steps, standing on his feet in our socks. Or he would twirl us around. It seemed the epitome of transcendent romance.

Titillating as all this was, it didn't jibe with another piece of family lore. What my father really wanted was a boy. My brother was born 10 years after me. If we were three puppies at the same feeding bowl, my brother was the crown prince. And we were expected to swallow this two-class system.

But it wasn't that simple. Despite my gender, my father had a limitless faith in me. Be anything you want to be, was his view. What better gift is there from a parent?

When I reached my 20s, there was yet another twist. He seemed to reconsider. Don't be too smart, too competitive, too opinionated; in short, too much like him. But it was too late for me to learn the art of playing the diminutive.

Then he was gone, leaving this array of contradictory messages to both hobble and inspire me. I have watched the fathers of friends give them away at their weddings, help them with a down payment on a house, see them become mothers and play with grandkids. I have friends who have consoled their fathers through divorce and stood ambivalently by through remarriage. I have seen my husband's father turn gray and frail.

Each time I traverse my loss again. He is still not here. The intransigence of death staggers the imagination. And so he surfaces again on Father's Day. ๑

13

b o b i e

I HAVE THIS CLUSTER OF THINGS I CARRY WITH ME FROM MY GRANDMOTHER.

One is in my jewelry box — a buttonhook for fastening those old-fashioned shoes, a bit of mother-of-pearl inlaid in the handle.

Others are in my memory, a pink-beaded dress, long gone, that my sisters and I used for playing dress-up. When one of us would put it on, we would imagine our grandmother as a "Charleston girl," a glamour woman, which she was not. She worked herself to the bone most of her life, she would tell us.

Then there was her hair, her glory. She had thick, white untamed curls framing her face. She always cut her hair herself. She never went to a beauty shop. A curl would get too wild, she would snip it off. It was her distinctive look, hair going every which way, long before it was fashionable.

Once I thought I saw my grandmother in a book of Lewis Hines photographs. As a 12-year-old immigrant child, she worked in a stogy factory. She was proud of it. But there, in a series on child labor in the early part of the century, was a photo of a row of girls in long dresses and button shoes rolling stogies in a factory in Pittsburgh's Hill District. I studied their faces to find my grandmother.

She was my only grandparent to grow old, to live into my adulthood. Because of her, I will always be drawn to the power of the immigrant story. She came here with her mother by boat after walking from a Polish village to a port in Germany. Her father was already here, earning the money to bring them over.

She worked side-by-side with my grandfather, running a small shop in a mill town outside of Pittsburgh. When his health failed in the 1940s, they left for California. They were pioneers, moving on whenever they needed.

She would visit in the summer. We thought some of her ways odd. In the morning, she ate a soft-boiled egg with a spoon out of the shell; in the evening, she drank warm milk diluted with hot water. At night her false teeth were in a glass in the bathroom. I would watch her, hand mirror held close, yank hairs out of her chin with tweezers.

She was not a fancy woman. She had a short, square body and toothpick legs. As an old woman, she wore tie shoes with block heels. When she sat in most chairs, her feet wouldn't reach the floor. But she was a powerful woman in her own way; she pulled her share.

She taught me to knit. I sat at her elbow struggling with my first scarf while she clicked along making a dress in dark turquoise. "Bobie, can you fix this?" I would implore after I had dropped yet another stitch. And she would.

She made a not-quite-triumphant return east when she could no longer live on her own. My mother moved her to a nursing home a few blocks from my house. I would visit; my two young children were hot items with the lonely women there.

One of the saddest moments was coming into the nursing home not long before she died and seeing that someone had done her hair. Her curls were flattened and tamed, her hair slick after being blown dry and sprayed. The nurse exclaimed how nice she looked. But to me she had lost something important of herself in yet one more way in this institution.

So many years later, how clearly I see the arc of her life. I have only a vague idea of her daily struggles and relationships, but I feel I know some essence of her distilled in this cluster of things.

She was a woman who wore button shoes and worked in a Pittsburgh stogy factory. She was a pioneer. She worked to the bone in the small shop in the town that once made steel. At one time she wore a pink-beaded dress. And she passed along her untamed curly hair and love of the color and texture of yarns. I know her in that cluster of things. ✦

15

16

b e l o n g i n g

AT THE AGE OF 50, MY FATHER TURNED AWAY FROM A SUCCESSFUL BUSINESS, WHICH HE HAD BEGUN 25 years before, to become a race-horse driver.

Friends and family were aghast at his decision. It did not fit anyone's idea of taking that serious turn into middle age. But then, for as long as I had known him, he had never been much concerned with "fitting anyone's idea." He went his own way.

What he saw was that he had grown up poor. He had never had a chance to pursue a sport. This was it. I don't know why he chose to live on the edge. But I do know that the way he was set us apart. It gave our family a cast of unconventionality.

It was not only in this single decision. My father did not put much stock in us learning the complicated and invisible rules of fitting in. As my sisters, brother and I entered school, we had the same passion to belong as most kids. His indifference, of course, did nothing to immunize us against those treacherous social waters.

Sitting alone at lunch, getting teased on the playground, not being picked for a team are private pains for most children. More often than not, it is beyond the reach of parents. It can be where, outside of the family, we form our earliest feelings about belonging — or not. Those hurts can leave their imprint long into adulthood.

My mother could be wound into the vagaries of popularity and having friends. My sister's elementary years were tainted by a tormentor named Eileen. I had my own difficulties with the taunts of girls in sixth grade.

My father seemed to lack the social antennae for these machinations. He was not only oblivious to these tribal struggles, he was impatient with them. He took the view that the whole matter of belonging was seriously overrated.

The issue was not how to get Eileen to be a friend, but why even bother. If she made it that difficult, how could it be worth it? More important in his mind was how to be yourself. Sometimes we felt he just didn't get it.

But the fact that he conceded nothing to the peer group meant that when we became teens, he still held all the cards. Our lament — "But everyone else is going" — held not an ounce of water with him.

When I had my own children, I had a whole new round with this matter of belonging and saw how many-sided it is. I was surprised by how attuned parents were to their children fitting in — from play dates to having the latest toys. It can make for a rather abrupt reversal in middle and high school, when suddenly you want your children to think for themselves and not be vulnerable to peer pressure.

As parents, we want the experiences of childhood to add up to an inner sense of belonging. We want our children to be able to move with ease and confidence in most situations. None of us wants a child to be left with a lasting sense of himself as an outsider, a loner or a misfit.

Perhaps I have grown into my father's skepticism. Belonging can become too much of an imperative. Feeling good that you belong can be predicated on excluding others. And it can demand a conformity that is stifling.

My father was not much consolation in the moment, but he gave me something more, a healthy suspicion of being engulfed by any group, institution or way of thinking. He taught me to make my own way with few labels. It took me many years to grow into it. Soon enough you have to stand on your own two feet. You might as well start that way. ᕲ

18

g r a n d p a r e n t s

EVERY SUNDAY WE HAD THIS RITUAL: MY FATHER WOULD TAKE MY TWO SISTERS AND ME
to our grandparents' for brunch. The clan would gather —
my father's aunts, uncles, cousins who since have had only a
dim place in my life. But the scene around that kitchen table
is still vivid. They spent hours eating, laughing, and talking
and arguing in Yiddish. My sisters and I barely understood a
word that was said.

The men smoked cigars and slammed their fists on the
table. The women, especially my grandmother, shuttled back
and forth bringing food from large pots on the stove.

We children slithered between the adults, having to endure
uncles pinching our cheeks, to find our places at the small,
yellow Formica table for the few minutes it took us to eat.
Then we were off to our own adventures in that dark, not
very child-friendly house. Their world was not accessible to
us. Nor ours to them.

By the time I was 10, both of these grandparents had died.
But those visits remain a reservoir of mystery and
enchantment to me.

My grandparents were unlike today's, who have Florida
retirement homes, Reeboks and AARP memberships. Mine
fled the Jewish ghetto of Kiev in the early part of the century.
They lived in their own ghetto here. They had their world
around that kitchen table. And there was the world in which
they struggled to survive.

I saw my father as fully Americanized, but in fact he
straddled both worlds. With his relatives, speaking only
Yiddish, he entered that other world.

My grandmother was short and round, her shapeless dresses
always covered by a flowered apron, her hair pulled straight
back. She loved her lilacs in the back yard. She was probably
only in her late 50s, but I thought of her as old.

After we ate, we were ignored, expected to fend for ourselves
for the afternoon. There were no toys, but we didn't care. We
invented nonsensical games out of thin air that we found
both hilarious and compelling.

At the kitchen table, we would rub our fingers on the plastic-
covered chairs, marveling at the magic of the spot turning
hot. We could not repress our giggles at our grandmother's
way of turning the spoon over and balancing it on the side of
the bowl when she served her chicken soup. Were we not
very secretly making fun of her old country ways?

We made endless pretend calls on the old-fashioned wall
phone, holding the quaint receiver to our ears and standing
on the tottery stool to reach the mouthpiece. And we rolled
ourselves silly on the hassocks in the living room.

As I grew, adult realities worked their way into my
consciousness, challenging and sometimes dissolving these
idealized images.

My memory of the house was as huge and exotic. But going
back several times as an adult, I was not able to identify it
with certainty and actually found the houses on the street
quite modest and prosaic.

I have also realized my mother was not along for what I
considered to be these most exciting excursions. Later I
learned she did not see eye-to-eye with her in-laws. I have
also heard of other family disputes, making me wonder about
the subject of discussion around that table.

Like most parents, mine, in due time, fell from that idealized
place in my mind. I soon was to feel ambivalence, anger,
guilt and obligation toward them, in addition to love.

But my grandparents have remained encapsulated behind
a gauzy veil, a safe haven of good feeling and acceptance.
And they are my only link to the old world. ✌

19

m o t h e r

WHEN MY MOTHER WAS IN HER 70s, SHE ASKED ME TO ACCOMPANY HER TO A BIG HOOPLA FOR HER college. It was an elaborate event to kick off the fund-raising campaign. The program was a high-powered, nostalgic musical revue, put on by the university's drama school. It was in a huge arena seating thousands, normally used for hockey games and rock concerts.

She hated crowds but she was keen to go to this. Our seats were near the top and she had to struggle to climb the steps to get to them. The alumni were seated by class. She greeted with buzzing excitement the other older women, her former classmates, seated in our section.

As I sat down, the woman on the other side of me said, "Now I hope you don't mind. I'm going to sing all the school songs."

And she did. Actually, she belted them out. So did my mother. Having gone to a different college, I was kind of out of it. But I was fascinated with my mother. In that evening of frenzied school spirit, I caught a fresh glimpse of her. Under all those layers charged for me with being my mother, I saw this free, expansive college girl.

My own college years were infused with a certain ambivalence about my mother. In fact, debunking mothers could have been practically classified as a leisure-time activity. In the dorm, we would sprawl on rumpled beds in the rubble of clothes and books and muse over our mothers.

The mother-admirers, and there were a few, lost interest in due time. But for the hard-core, it was a compelling activity. There was a kind of romance in proclaiming our lack of fit, a definite bonding among us in this self-orphaning.

I remember classifying women, whether friends, celebrities or heroines in novels, in two groups: Those who got along with their mothers and those who didn't. When I would meet someone, it was as if I had this antenna out. It would pick up on those on the outside and those who I saw as still in the cocoon.

I was skeptical of those whose relationships with their mothers seemed to be smooth sailing. Was it just a conventional, unquestioned acceptance? And I glamorized those who didn't get along with their mothers. They were interesting, rebellious. Wasn't that what college was all about?

At the core of these discussions was always that great philosophical question: Was a good relationship with one's mother possible? Of course, it was only a rhetorical question.

Not that any of us had a real bill of particulars. For the life of me, I can't remember exactly what was so very wrong with all those mothers. As for me, my mother and I had no memorable conflagrations.

No, this simmering stew was not about any argument or having different views on this or that. It was this pervasive and stifling feeling that their very presence kept us from being ourselves.

Ironically, as I look back on those years, I think of it as a time when, in all that angst, I became the person I wanted to be. Mother rumination was part of it. We were trying to put together the sometimes inadequate, sometimes contradictory pieces that comprise being female.

At one moment we held them responsible for the sorry state of womankind. At another, we seemed on a quest for the good mother, not only the one we had, but the one we hoped to find in ourselves.

That night at the college fete, I saw a view of my mother that made me feel an unexpected bond with her. Lit only in the shadows of the spotlights, I could see in her happy face a time in her life when she too had shed a cocoon and, like me, had become the person she wanted to be. ◈

independence

WHAT EXACTLY WAS THE BIG DEAL, I HAVE THOUGHT MANY TIMES OVER THE years. All I wanted was my own apartment. You would have thought I had committed a crime. Or, at the very least, had turned my back on them, my parents, in some brutal, unfeeling way.

I was 22, not 16. I had lived away from home in high school and college, then at home for a year after I graduated. I had a good job. I wanted my own place.

It was the mid-'60s. I was not calling for the overthrow of the social order. Just their social order. What I wanted, it seemed, was even more revolutionary.

The night I left was like a divorce. My mother's face was stricken as she stood helplessly watching me carry things to the car. My father was upstairs. His absence, his aloofness from this moment of rupture, I mean departure, only heightened his thundering disapproval.

Suddenly my mother was galvanized, opening drawers and stuffing a couple of tablecloths into a bag. "Here, take these," she said, putting the bag into my hands.

What did I need with tablecloths? I didn't even have a table. I took them anyway. Oh, parents and their insufferable need to be helpful.

I could see, even then, that they could not help themselves. They were caught in changing times. I was not divorcing them. I was simply having my own life. I drove off into the dark — clothes, books and tablecloths in the car — to my one-room apartment one mile away.

It wasn't that women in the mid-'60s didn't live on their own. But most carried it off with more finesse. They had the grace to move to another city to carry on their independence. They did the socially accepted thing of going to college and not coming back. I was making my declaration right under their noses.

You cannot imagine the upheaval. In our first talk after my announcement, my father was the point man. She had put him up to it. Bring out the heavy artillery. She was too upset to look at me. You would have thought I had joined the Weathermen.

They took it very personally. Did I not find them interesting? Had they not provided adequate accommodations? More to the point, what life did I want to lead anyway that I couldn't under their roof?

Not that I was having an easy time of it. In this fray, I turned to a friend at work and asked, how actually do you get your own apartment? Matter-of-factly, he pointed the way out of this emotional thicket: Pick up the classifieds, call a few places, visit, make a decision and put down a deposit.

So what was the big deal? It was never spoken, mind you, but the point was this: I belonged to them until I belonged to someone else.

There was only one way to legitimately move out of the house: Get married. My older sister did at 19, my younger one at 20. Never mind that she divorced a few years later.

Like walking on the moon or fax machines or in-vitro fertilization, a daughter with her own space and her own life was not an arrangement they had ever imagined.

They settled in. Did they have a choice? I visited often. In truth, I missed them. But each time I would get ready to leave, my living arrangement once again wouldn't add up for them. Why aren't you here with us was the unspoken question. I thought my mother might thrust tablecloths at me again.

Not long after the night of our divorce, my father extended the olive branch. He arrived at my new apartment one day in a truck with the bookshelves from my old room, a table and lamps. I felt as if I were Red China getting recognized.

I still have all of those things. In fact, I would never part with any of them. When I look at them, I am reminded of my emancipation and my connection. ❧

23

s a r a h

EVERY TIME I PASSED THE BOXES STACKED NEATLY IN THE BASEMENT, I WOULD BE REMINDED that I had not unpacked them yet. About 10 in all, they were filled with dishes, glasses, pottery, odds and ends of kitchen implements. The last remnant of my in-laws' household.

Last year we moved my husband's father here from Pittsburgh. Soon after, my husband and his sister closed down the house. Many of the things were caked with dust; they hadn't been touched since my mother-in-law Sarah had died 13 years ago.

It was not just a matter of finding a chunk of time to do the job. I was waiting for the right mood to revisit the complicated feeling I knew I would encounter for the woman reflected in those things.

There are times when a relationship is so powerful it seems your life suddenly ignites and takes off. One moment you're stalled and struggling with no result. Then all of a sudden the pieces fit together and there's a way to go forward.

Meeting my husband was like that. But he had a bonus tucked away I'm not sure he even fully appreciated. Sarah and I clicked. So much for the popular myths about mothers-in-law.

I was in my mid-20s when we met, still a renegade from my own mother. I was "struggling to find myself" as the expression went. With soft-spoken Sarah, I found congruence. We would talk. Mostly, she would listen.

She took me in as I was. She didn't focus on what I wasn't. No admonitions, no campaigns for improvement.

To me she had cachet because she was so unadorned and straightforward. Short and round, she wore her waist-length hair in a braid wrapped around her head. Some of her ways were even backward. She didn't drive, so she walked to get her groceries nearly every day. She had no dishwasher and used an old-fashioned wringer-washer.

But in other ways she was thoroughly modern and relevant. She was a social worker in a hi-tech hospital, working with kidney dialysis patients in the early days of its availability. She supervised students and over the years developed a wide circle of admirers. Many looked to her for counsel, even some of my friends. I felt so lucky having the honored daughter-in-law position.

But altruism was only one side of Sarah. She was big on just having fun. She would laugh until tears ran down her cheeks. She loved to dance. She would take us to see a magic show or an acrobatic group.

She loved Elvis Presley.

She would take the kids overnight. They'd play office with old papers, deposit slips and stampers she had gathered. When we came to pick them up, she would look like an exhausted but happy camp counselor.

She loved to make a party. Any reason would do. She'd make a Valentine's cake and get the kids to decorate. She'd fuss over one of her special dishes and put candles on the dinner table. And she'd coo over her own creations even though it might be a simple chicken dish.

Last weekend my husband and I unwrapped everything he had so carefully packed in newspaper and ran it all through the dishwasher. Her plain white china, her green and yellow mixing bowls, her good bread knife, the beautiful handmade pottery that reflected her warmth and simple tastes.

When I met her, I was unformed. I was hungry for female figures to make my own. And I rejected most that came my way. She took me under her wing. And I made my peace with being female.

We found a place for nearly everything in drawers or on the shelves. It made me remember how she had taken me in. ॐ

25

d i s h e s

ONLY ONCE HAVE I HURLED A KITCHEN OBJECT IN ANGER. AND IT HAPPENED TO BE PLASTIC.

I was emptying the dishwasher. It doesn't matter whom I was angry at or why. You probably understand, anyway. Let's say I had met with a disappointment in the appreciation category.

I lit upon a juice container and flung it to the floor. To my surprise it bounced, landing unscathed on the counter. No attrition. But no satisfaction either in having smashed anything. Not even this once. Pretty disappointing for someone as slow as me to fire. But then, I do come by this naturally, the propensity to invest high-intensity emotion in domestic objects. For years I watched my mother's many moods reflected in how she handled dishes.

At times, they gave her the pleasure of a female adornment, almost like pretty clothes or fancy jewelry. For company or holidays, she would be happily ensconced among her dishes, pulling out ones we rarely saw from out-of-reach cupboards and arranging them just so on the dining room table.

Her everyday dishes — white with a blue pattern — were like a large fan she spread out in an even rhythm each day gathering us in, binding us to her and to each other.

She was most approachable when she was "doing dishes." If there was something important, private to say to her, it was best said as we scraped plates or while handing her hot dishes to put away from the dishwasher.

Dishes had a dark side for her, too. My mother could take the love-me, love-my-food stance. If we disrespected her meals or fought at the table, you could see her anger take shape in the way she moved dishes about. It might be an extra thrust or twist in her wrist when she set a dish down on the table or a bowl in the sink. Unlike me, she occasionally broke some. The dishes were the repository of her mood.

Dishes have a way of binding one generation of women to another. Men pass down their names, property, even their businesses. Women pass down dishes, literally and figuratively in this whole complicated business of feeding.

Even the artist Judy Chicago chose to tell the history of women, beginning with goddesses, through plates in her controversial piece called "The Dinner Party."

It took me a long time to be ready to take my place in this chain. When I married I boldly declared, "No dishes for a wedding gift," hoping to shuck that heritage of gathering together and feeding that seemed to me at the time to so ensnare womankind.

Little did I know in the years ahead how many times I would handle the same dishes. Now, more than 20 years later, it seems I have grown into a person who can't have too many of them.

Where once I had a few odd plates and cereal bowls, I now, like my mother, have sets and parts of sets squirreled away in the kitchen cupboards, dishes for everyday and for holidays. I can't imagine divesting myself of any of them.

I have inherited my mother's good dinner plates now, white with green leaves around the border, a few of them chipped. I use them only occasionally, but when I do, I can feel her pleasure in handling them.

So as dishes have gradually filled my cupboards, they have taken on this evocative power, perhaps something of my mother's many moods. ❧

f a m i l y   p h o t o

OUT OF THE BLUE, A PHOTOGRAPH FROM MY CHILDHOOD APPEARED IN THE MAIL THE OTHER DAY. There we were: my mother, my two sisters and me.

My younger sister, Rita, sent it. She said she came across it when she was cleaning a long-untouched area of her house. I was startled to be faced with this artifact after so many years, this small black-and-white with scalloped edges, containing the group of us standing in front of a summer cottage.

My mother is in the center, smiling slightly. The three of us have the same dark, curly hair, all cut a little below our ears, all parted on one side and held back with a barrette or hairband. My older sister, Anne, who looks to be about 10, is on one side of my mother. Rita, probably 5, is standing in front of her. I, likely 8, am on my mother's left, holding her hand, which is affectionately around my shoulder.

Childhood photos have a compelling quality. When we become adults, we piece together our own version of growing up. Some of it is remembered. Some we know in our bones. But the pictures are irrefutable proof of what was there. We hold onto the ones that are in alignment with what we know.

This photo was one I had never seen, probably because Rita had had it for years. I don't know about your family, but in mine, we siblings carried out a certain ransacking of the family photos.

They were kept stashed in boxes in a random fashion. On visits home, we would pull out these boxes and sift through them. Somehow each of us felt the liberty, even entitlement, to take the ones in which we figured most prominently or that we found most flattering. Or that fit our version of the way things were. I guess Rita laid claim to this one because she is standing in the front, smiling and looking pretty cute.

Even though over the years I, too, had taken the ones I wanted, an unsettling thing happened after both of my parents were gone. Suddenly I was deluged with photos. I wound up with all of my baby pictures. I found that I wanted to forever think of my parents as the repository of my childhood. Getting those photos made me feel they had up and quit. I may have struggled a good part of my young adult life to let go of them. Then, the way it turned out, they let go of me.

So when this photo arrived the other day, I was taken aback. I thought I had seen all the photos there were to see. Looking at it, I felt momentarily hurled back into our configuration, hooked in again to the richness and to the hot rivalries that we have managed to cool down and smooth away after all these years. I found myself studying every detail. The one I found most riveting was the way in which my mother had her arm around me. I could not help wondering: Where had this picture been all of my life?

It wasn't that I hadn't felt loved by my mother. But over the years, I have often joked to Rita that, between the two of them, it's no wonder I got so little air time. I would offer as proof that, in the family photos, I could not recall any that showed my mother and me in an affectionate relation to one another.

So here it was. It came as if in answer to my years of joking. OK, maybe half-joking. It was a long time in coming, but yes, in a funny, literal way, it felt like some final and indisputable proof. I was touched that she saw fit to part with it and send it my way. ❧

s i s t e r s

"WE'RE HAVING DINNER TOGETHER," MY YOUNGER SISTER TOLD ME WHEN I BROUGHT up the matter of our older sister's birthday a few days away.

I winced, imagining their cozy party. I'm not proud to admit it, but I felt left out. How could they be getting together without me?

Actually, quite easily. They both live in New York, not a half-hour from each other. Here I am in Cleveland, a prohibitive air fare away, especially with a last-minute decision.

It is not that they had excluded me. If I had said I wanted to come, I am sure both of them would have said, "By all means, come. In fact, please come, we would love to have you."

Still, something about the thought of their dinner violated our configuration, the old configuration that had so imprinted us. I was in the middle, the hinge between the two of them. They, at least until recent years, were less connected to each other. So, as I said, how could they be getting together without me?

Because we had long outgrown all of that, left that old configuration behind. I was a cheerleader for leaving our old, somewhat calcified ways behind. I am sure they were, too. So we could be ourselves.

How complicated the labyrinth of sisters is, especially with only five years in age separating the three of us. Siblings are touted for their love of, loyalty to and sharing with each other. But three is such an unstable number. When two fall out, there's always someone to confide in. Before we were old enough to know ourselves, we were well-schooled in the less desirable traits of jealousy, hoarding and betrayal. We have our stories — the blue skirt, freely given, then taken back.

And I haven't even mentioned the brother, much younger, another family really, definitely another story.

As for the three of us, we have evolved over the years. The big sister shed the place of prerogative. The baby sister gave up the spot of special care and attention. And I, in the middle, shaped by everyone else's wishes, gave up the spineless, fruitless job of mediator. That is, we more or less gave these things up.

For so long, it seemed we were held captive by what went on back then. Perhaps it is not until there are no parents anymore, as it is for us, that the juice goes out of those old struggles. The parents were who brought us together. They were also who kept us apart. They unwittingly fueled our machinations.

When parents are gone, you are free to step away from the old configuration or step away altogether. When parents are gone, you also see that it is siblings who are there to go on with, who know you longer than anyone. So we try to just be ourselves. It is not always easy. We are, it turns out, quite different from one another.

In some sense the older sister will always be the one I watched leading the way to school on the first day, as I hung back holding my mother's hand, whom I followed to bicycles, boys and babies.

And the younger sister will always be the repository for my emotional heat. She would say, "See you on the phone," when we would pull away in the car from our summer visits with her family. Our time to talk was not possible with husbands and kids around.

So, yes, the old configuration has loosened its grip. Just not completely. I can still feel, even for a moment, the pull of that cozy place in the middle at the birthday dinner table. ❧

the cleaner

WHENEVER THOSE SURVEYS COME OUT BERATING HUSBANDS FOR MAKING ONLY INFINITESIMAL progress in taking up their share of the housework, I feel proud — but also a little sheepish.

You see, my husband is exemplary. He is off the charts. He is a credit to his gender.

His forte is cleaning, and he does it so well, there is no way I could keep up. He leaves me in the dust, so to speak.

But before you grab a pen to write where you can get a clone, I must clarify. The wellspring for this is not any great sense of our equality. He knows he is superior in this area. He cleans and straightens because he must. We live in a very tidy house. Very little of it is my doing.

Unbelievably, I have actually had some trouble learning to live with this. Much as I carry the flag for equality, somehow, deeply ingrained in my soul is the idea that cleaning, maybe half of it, is the female lot.

Of all the arguments for living together before marriage, one of the strongest is to unearth the strange ways of your beloved, to pinpoint those places where you are not one and where you would never wish to be.

What I am talking about here is the perplexing dichotomies that emerge in a relationship where you are hopelessly out of sync: He is a morning person, you a night person; he sees the glass half-full, you half-empty. And of course, there is the neat freak and the slovenly one.

I prefer a certain amount of casual clutter: Kicked-off shoes in front of the couch are fine; so is the toothpaste tube left out on the bathroom sink. After all, it's not a museum. We want some evidence that people — nice, easygoing people — live here. Not so for my husband. I believe he lives with a fear that, left to my own devices, we would be overrun. It is

his mission, therefore, to stamp out any early warning signs of disarray. So he straightens bathroom towels stuffed hurriedly on the rack, closes closet doors, hangs coats that have been tossed across the banister.

We are simply calibrated differently. His constant tidying makes me feel constricted, confined, stifled. He is simply unhinged if things get too messy.

The dishwasher seems to cry out to him. He empties it just because it's full! I don't see the point unless a new load is building in the sink. When cooking, I may root around for the stirring spoon, only to find he has already put it in the dishwasher.

And he's not always a silent butler. He takes a certain delight in presuming we are just ahead of the deluge. He will gleefully hold up a cucumber on the verge of liquefying or a leftover that has grown a fur coat. He will "tsk tsk" at the suggestion of going to bed when dirty pots are still in the kitchen sink.

It can put me on the brink. Suddenly Tina Turner's "What's Love Got to Do With It?" is blaring in my head.

For years I felt inadequate, that I was not the proper wife. I could never keep up. I didn't even want to. Then I learned. I had only to look in the eyes of my women friends. They were incredulous. You don't get it, they said. Relax.

So I laid down the burden that says cleaning is the prerogative of my gender. Gradually, he has taken control of policing nearly all areas of the house.

I do have one sanctuary left, a chair in the bedroom for clothes I don't, at the moment, feel like hanging up. But I fear he may be planning a spring offensive. ✺

33

halloween brothers

FOR MY FIRST SON, LOUIS, HALLOWEEN WAS A TWO-PRONGED EVENT INVOLVING both character and candy. Weeks ahead he would decide whom he wanted to be — for years it seemed he was fixed on Groucho Marx. Hyped up, he would want to go early and with a sturdy bag. With his gang of friends, he would move along at a good clip so that by the end of the evening, the bag had heft to it, surely enough candy to last well into November. Even at 5, 6 years old, he was practical, strategic, focused.

For Max, my second son, the holiday was an entirely different experience. Through his early childhood, he played from a box of props, moving in and out of different characters. A decorated cardboard tube was Robin Hood's quiver; a green towel pinned to the shoulders of his shirt made him Batman's Robin; two baseball caps, one turned forward, one back, and he was Sherlock Holmes. He played knight, soldier, Indian. (In fact, he had an Indian period during which he slept in a tepee in the hall.)

In a way, Halloween was his holiday. Choosing whom to be was complicated. It might be the culmination of months of an evolving character or a new one he was just trying out.

Then there was the titillating fear of that bewitched night. He would be transfixed by the rustling leaves, the shadows of trees made by the streetlights, the huddles of masked kids coming toward him. It was as if the whole dark, spooky scene was precisely choreographed.

The candy was not exactly incidental. He wanted a hefty bag at evening's end, especially when he saw his brother's. It was just that he was too caught up in being someone other than himself, in a magical world other than his own, to focus on what he needed to do to get it.

Taking the two of them out was something short of enchantment for me. It was a logistical nightmare. Louis would zoom ahead, running up steps, greeting people cheerfully, looking for shortcuts to the next house. He would be halfway down the block and Max would still be looking for the goblins in the bushes, with one lollipop in his bag.

Of course, by the time they were old enough to go Halloweening, I was already well-versed in their separate worlds. Louis began life with a piercing, insistent cry. It was as if he were saying, make things right — and now. Being that he was my first, I was obedient. Once he was taken care of, he would be off crawling, walking, exploring, conquering, hardly looking back.

Nineteen months later came serene Max. He slowed me down. He dallied in feeding, enjoying the pleasure of being enveloped by the whole ambience of it.

Each new situation brought a new variation to their differences. To Louis, an amusement park was a challenge, a dare. He wanted to cover every ride and the scarier, the better. To Max, the rides were scary. He would move slowly, taking in all the details of the raucous carnival atmosphere.

When they had a lemonade stand in the summer, Louis was the organizer, keeping track of the cups, lemonade, ice and money. But he was shy and tongue-tied when it came to customers. Max loved to engage them. It was yet another role, that of storekeeper.

But Halloween was that quintessential moment when I would be forced to ponder: How could my own two children, of the same gender, in the same family and with the same parents, be so utterly different? ❧

35

36

c o o l

IT'S A MOMENT I WILL NOT FORGET. IT WAS MY OLDER SON'S EIGHTH GRADE GRADUATION. Unlike his male classmates who had gone along with donning dark suits and ties, he had insisted on wearing a casual, wrinkly, pale, blue cotton, sport jacket and striped shirt.

Still, my heart swelled with the strains of "Pomp and Circumstance." Then I caught a glimpse of him coming down the auditorium aisle: No tie, collar open and the shirttails hanging out below the jacket!

Did I mention that his head was shaved on one side? It was the days of the asymmetrical look. I can't remember — I actually may be blocking on this — his initials may have been carved in the hair of the shaved side of his head. It was a certain look he was after, he explained later. This event was where he had decided to make his statement. And it worked; he was the hit of graduation.

The issue, of course, was being cool. You won't find it in Dr. Spock and it doesn't even warrant a chapter in child development textbooks. But some time, likely in middle school, cool — getting it and keeping it — will become the most consuming endeavor of your child's life. It's so absorbing that it's a wonder he ever gets anything else done. Actually, for a few years there some don't.

Cool just starts cropping up. One day you find him pinning the bottoms of those nice pants you bought him because he thinks the legs are too wide. And shoes. All of a sudden it has to be high tops, untied shoelaces and expensive. Hair is given over to cool whether it means long and loose, a ponytail, spiked-up or the box.

You no sooner get with the shoes and the hair and it's the boxers hanging out below the shorts or the jeans halfway down the backside. One day a flowered Hawaiian shirt becomes imperative. Or a pro-team jacket.

Cool is a look. It's a walk. It's an attitude. It's what kind of music you listen to. There's no faster way for one kid to dismiss another than to discover they are not into the same bands.

Cool is irrepressible, mysterious, unpredictable. If you dare to mention that expensive Hawaiian shirt after its time has passed, you'll hear, "Oh that's for geeks."

Cool makes going shopping together a nightmare. All you have to do is touch a shirt on the rack and say, "This is nice," and you have contaminated it.

Parents, you're left in the dust. You can't keep up, you're bewildered. In short, you're clueless, the epitome of uncool. Make no mistake, once cool starts to make its presence felt, it is the line in the sand between the generations.

You may find all this superficial. But don't be deceived by appearances. If our kids could just speak to us, and of course they can't, I know they say that an adult is getting born somewhere in this chaos of cool.

I know because, in fact, my son grew through this. His cool cooled down to a simpler look. He has a short, symmetrical haircut. He wears a rather drab uniform of worn, gray clothes, made so because he washes everything together. The shoes are work boots. The jeans are baggy and the few holes are considered good.

But in those days when cool was hot, fellow parents passed along this balm: Save the fight for the big ones. Hair, clothes, music — hey, that's the little stuff.

So I say, as a seasoned mother of two sons, when the cool starts to flow — be cool. Hang in there, put up the good fight knowing you will likely lose. Be glad if he doesn't make his stand on graduation day.

Girls, you say? The hair, the makeup, the nails, let alone the attitude — now that's a cool that is way beyond me. ❧

HE WAS ALWAYS THE HARD-LINER, I THE SOFT TOUCH. WHEN OUR TWO BOYS, growing up, wanted to stay up a little later, have an extra snack, not clean up right then because they were too tired, they came to me, whining, begging, charming, irresistible.

It's not that I wasn't for discipline and learning right from wrong. It's just that at certain moments the letter of the law had a kind of hollow ring to it. Rules were fine as long as you could bend them when they didn't quite fit.

But my husband saw it quite differently. He stood for toeing the line, for consequences. A no was a no. No negotiation. Sometimes I even resorted to a little subterfuge. Maybe someone didn't do so well on a school paper, got into a fight, broke something. I might not make too much of it, if it came up. And if it didn't, well, it didn't.

So we stumbled along, Yin and Yang, at best a balance for each other — more likely, a jumbled package of freedom and discipline, individuality and conformity, forgiveness and criticism. It was at times the very antithesis of that textbook "united front" held up to parents as essential to producing that good model citizen.

At worst, we got in each other's hair. I can remember arguing my case, feeling as though it came from deep within the trenches of who I was. And if you asked him, I am sure he would recall an equal force to his convictions.

I would say: This is how they learn, he's just a kid, don't be so harsh. He would say: Make a decision and stick by it.

I thought he was rigid. He thought I was wishy-washy, muddying up the moral waters.

I thought he was a spoilsport, not in favor of any fun. He thought I spoiled them.

He was horrified that we presented such an inconsistent picture. I was horrified at the mountains he made out of what seemed molehills.

It made the air in the house quite thick at times. The bubble of romantic oneness had definitely popped. I remember wondering what people with no children ever had to disagree over.

But over the years, something very strange happened. Imperceptibly, we seem to have each taken a long journey, arriving exactly at each other's positions.

I, the libertarian of this two-party system, am suddenly the house conservative. I find myself saying about one child or the other: Shouldn't we enforce some consequences to such-and-such a deed, will he ever get his act together, why should he consider being so far away from home?

And my law-and-order husband pleads their cases: Let him go where he wants, he's going through a little period of rebellion, let him make his own decisions, let him make his own mistakes, don't make him feel guilty, keep the lines of communication open.

I think he may be soft in the head. He thinks that I'm uptight and that I am getting distressed over molehills.

Now, with our children away from home, he too is having long confidential phone conversations with them.

But we are better at it now. We give each other a lot of slack and even a little respect. There's no pretense at a united front. By now they know for sure we are two very different people.

But I wonder: Was there something in being a mother of young children that he simply could not be part of, a love so powerful that bending the rules was not a compromise, but just being human?

And is there something, too, about being the father of young men that I cannot be part of, a love so powerful that it contains the permission, no, the affirmation and excitement for going out into the world and claiming it as one's own? ❧

39

40

s o c c e r

IT IS SUPPOSED TO BE HIS YEAR. THAT'S THE WAY HE HAS SEEN IT. HE SAT ON THE BENCH, PAYING his dues, playing only when the other goalkeeper was injured. Now the guy whom he loyally warmed up and patiently watched for two years has graduated.

It is his shot. He has worked for it. But it doesn't always work that way.

There's a new kid on the block. He struts out onto the soccer field making an unanticipated contest materialize out of thin air. The coach may be swayed by his flash. The image of the bench looms. Dreams threaten to vaporize.

One of my enduring images of my son Louis is as the ultimate defender, prowling in front of the goal, up on his toes, hunched over in the ready position, every inch of him alert.

He spent much of his teens honing himself as a goalkeeper. In turn, soccer carried him through adolescence, giving him an anchor, an outlet for his high energy and competitiveness.

His body is hard and muscular from training every day. Even though I spent years protecting him from harm, he's now often icing a shoulder, wearing a brace on a knee, having to tape a thumb. Around 15, he decided he wanted to "look more intimidating." So he cut his hair short. The end of his beautiful curls.

Guarding that 8-feet-high and 24-feet-across goal is one of the ways he has chosen to plant himself in the world. I often wonder, when I watch him play, what is in his character that made him choose a position where he faces the onslaught of a whole team, where he is the bottom line. When they win, it's a victory for all of them. But when they lose, even if no one has scored, he takes it as his loss. What a responsibility.

I used to think, it's just a game. But I have learned that soccer touches him at the deepest level. What any parent would want a child to learn about hard work, discipline, commitment, courage, teamwork and striving has been shaped by his engagement with this sport.

When he was younger, my fantasies about his future did not include goalkeeping. My image was more of a quiet, slender, bookish boy playing the cello. But at 11, he rejected Saturday afternoon cello lessons for soccer practice.

He had little to encourage him in his passion. When he entered high school, it did not even have a varsity team. So he taught himself. He learned to "make saves" by throwing himself onto a gym mat in the basement. Later, with his paper route money, he rented a small gym at a nearby church to practice.

He dreamed of tending goal for a select team that would take him to regional and state tournaments and on to college soccer. He despaired that he might never be good enough, and even if he was, how would he ever be discovered? The only team he had to play on was an amateurish one in the neighborhood.

But he persevered and got his shot. The day he tried out for a select team, I could see his focus and aggressiveness surge to meet the competition. I thought it might have been decisive in his making the team.

I wonder if that quality will be there for him now? And will it be enough?

I would do anything for him not to have to learn these bitter life lessons: A game that is supposed to be about fairness is not always fair. Hard work does not mean you will be rewarded. You can be valued, and yet you can be disposable.

But, of course, there is no way to protect him.

If he plays, I will be there cheering wildly when he makes a save. And I will ache for him if he misses, not so much for the losing but because I want his striving to be rewarded.

But most of all, I want him to get his shot. ໓

41

young women

IT'S A SLOW TRICKLE NOW, BUT WITH ANY LUCK IT COULD BECOME A REGULAR OCCURRENCE: MY TWO sons have been arriving home with lovely young women in tow.

After more than 20 years of being the lone female in my household, girls — or I should say young women — are finally seeping in.

I find them riveting. Last year at Thanksgiving, one son arrived with Meredith. She was warm, poised, interested, interesting. Even though our encounter was brief, I have to say I liked everything about her. I was ready to settle in.

Meredith's in Texas now, in another relationship and this son is seeing someone else, too. Clearly, I was more ready for a long-term relationship than either of them.

But then I have a certain amount of pent-up demand for these nervous, on-their-best-behavior female visitors. Having them come my way has made me realize I've been on a starvation diet for in-house female companionship. It's like suddenly feeling famished when you catch a whiff of wonderful food.

It's not that I haven't loved having boys. But there are some things mine, as yet, don't do. Like hang around and tune in, in the kitchen. It's not that I didn't try to involve them. It just didn't take. Sure they'd help, but usually they were in a hurry to get on with their own activity.

Having boys, in fact, was like getting put down in some exotic land of perpetual motion. They were practically born with little motors inside that "hrrmm hrmmed" with different variations of trains or racing cars. They'd use their bodies as torpedoes, throwing themselves to the ground. Fun was wrestling and getting pinned until you squealed, A novel kind of intimacy, I thought.

Joy was in racing a bike fast, knocking down a tower of blocks, sending up a rocket. A good day was walking to the fire station or a construction site. Or watching a garbage truck. They would collect objects for thrusting and poking and carry out elaborate enactments of Star Wars, knights, army or rescue.

It was a whole new world for me. I had moments of looking wistfully at friends with daughters. They'd be making frilly dresses as I put patches on knees of pants. Their daughters had shiny hair to be braided. I had to lure mine to the bath with toy submarines. Their girls would snuggle up to listen to our conversations, while my boys were busy zooming cars on the floor.

For years I have had this recurring question: When does all of this motion end? Only now do I have an answer. When they begin arriving home with young women.

This year my other son appeared with shy, serious Jessica, also thoroughly likable. In no time, she was leaning across the kitchen counter on her elbows, picking up the spoon to stir as I reached for the next ingredient. Where have you been all this time, I wondered.

This son told me something that made me pause: Jessica's parents think he is a wonderful influence on their daughter. Not that I doubt it. But it made me realize the weight I feel from his struggles. And how free I feel of hers. Clearly, her parents see it the other way.

Some of the pleasure is in these young women coming into my life. But it's also that they are already semi-finished products. It's other parents who have logged the years carrying the baggage.

I'm looking for this trickle to become a steady stream, and in time, return visits. ❧

43

g r a d u a t i o n

FOR SOMEONE LIKE ME, WHO CAN FIND THE DARK SIDE TO ALMOST ANYTHING, THERE ARE few experiences I would describe as unmitigated joy. Seeing an offspring graduate from college is one of them.

Ordinarily, I'm not drawn to formality or ritual. But I loved every moment of the pomp and pageantry of my son Louis' graduation.

Excuse me — Lou. That's his name now. One of his friends asked, "Who's Louis?" after hearing me address him a few times.

College is a wonderful invention. It's a moratorium when, no longer a kid and not yet an adult, you can molt and become the person you wish to be. Hence Lou. It seems an extraordinary privilege in this day, when kids much younger and in other circumstances are being tried in court as adults or are already carrying the full burden of parenthood.

You don't want too many details on senior week, those days of final fling leading up to graduation. A time to "hook up" (and this has a very particular meaning on college campuses) with anyone you may have even remotely flirted with in the past four years. A time to sit in the sun and say good-byes. And to party, party, party, all the while more or less awash in alcohol.

Then comes the inundation of parents. It's a strange feeling to be a guest of your kid, to be taken care of at his place. Lou made the dinner reservations; he and his friends handled all the arrangements. We followed along. This is the same kid who lost his keys three times the day we left him as a freshman.

There he was, a man, introducing us to his friends, and they, in turn, introducing us to their parents. It was kind of cozy, all these adults, with the generation gap disappearing before our eyes.

Except that we were suddenly old. He would drop us off after an evening out around 11 — a respectable time. Then he would go out with his friends. The next morning, in fine form, he would tell us, as he wolfed down a king-sized breakfast, that he had been out until 4. And to think we used to get a baby-sitter for him so we could go out.

This university graduated nearly 6,000. It was a perfect, clear, sunny day. Heightened anticipation filled the air as people gathered from all directions and moved toward the stadium where the ceremony was held. Then the band began to play full tilt. It took nearly 45 minutes for the black-robed faculty and graduates to file in. I was captivated the entire time.

From high in the stadium, the moving mass of robes and mortarboards looked like a swarm of ants. But I was able to spot my ant. Did I mention he was wearing a dark brown cowboy hat, instead of the mortarboard? At least it had a tassel hanging down the side.

The university president gave a great speech — funny, stirring and short. He was applauded wildly. As the procession out of the stadium began, it seemed as if the graduates were shot triumphantly out into the world.

I felt a pride like no other. This was so completely his accomplishment. Sure, we raised him. Sure, we paid for it. But he did it. He did it all on his own.

There's another reason for parents to attend graduation, other than to strut like peacocks. It's a marking point. It's a closure to an aspect of parenting. You can actually feel it. It's important not to miss it.

We walked along, part of the dispersing throng. Photo groupings formed everywhere. My husband put his arm around me and said, "You did a good job."

"You did, too," I said. It was a moment of unmitigated joy. ❧

45

leaving home

LATE AUGUST MEANS ANTICIPATION, BUILT INTO US AS CHILDREN DURING THOSE YEARS OF making the trek for new shoes that launched us into fall.

Then comes September, the month of fresh purposes. And new levels of separation, testing once again the elasticity of family bonds.

My older son graduated from college in the spring. So I thought perhaps I, too, might have graduated from the ranks of the September bereaved, those marked with the particular brand of Angst that comes with departures that get more distant each year.

But no such luck. This year will top all previous ones. This son is leaving today to spend the next 10 months working in a foreign land. I want to add right off that it was I who encouraged him to do this. Of course, it will be a wonderful experience and you will learn so much, I had said. But that was in the abstract, way back in winter.

Now it's real. That's perhaps why the thought of his leaving is sitting in me like an empty thud, carrying with it a faint element of rejection even though there is none. Such are feelings of loss.

Remember that ad, "It's 11 p.m. Do you know where your children are?"

What's popping up in my mind is slightly different: "It's August. Have I made peace with where this son will be?"

It has occurred to me recently that of the myriad threads that make up the complicated relationship between a parent and child, one aspect is simply spatial. Being a mother is part of what anchors me in the universe. I experience my relation to my sons as a kind of orbital pull. As they have grown, the force field has widened again and again.

Each step of the way, for a time, sets off some internal reshuffling, an adjustment to this new spatial relationship. Whether September brings kindergarten or college, the change, at least for a time, is a disruption, a loss until a new equilibrium is reached.

I'm not there yet. To date, I have only settled for a distance of six hours by car, the time it takes to get to his former university. I have not made my peace with a six-hour time difference, and as yet no address. I don't even know how long it takes for a letter to arrive there.

This moving away begins almost at the beginning. It is only during the first six months that they stay where you put them. From the time they can push off your lap and crawl across the room, your relationship in space is subject to constant expansionist pressure. In no time they are up on their feet, intoxicated with their own ability to move. We applaud and take pictures of those first steps, rejoicing in their accomplishment.

Riding a bicycle is another milestone of mobility. One minute you're having a near-heart attack running alongside, holding up your child on a two-wheeler, and suddenly they're on their own, careening away, the front wheel going every which way. That force field is widening again.

But that's nothing compared to the driver's license. Or leaving home.

Of course there's a down side to all this mobility. Each step is a step into their own trajectory. Each step away diminishes the intimacy.

A friend recently said to me, the 20s are the time to run the leash out as far as it will go.

So once again it looks as though I will be joining the ranks of the September bereaved. After all, our bond has to stretch halfway around the world now.

In time, as I have done many times in the past, I know I will settle on a new sense of him, in his new place, unknown as it is to me now. ❧

47

OUR SON HAD BEEN OUT OF THE COUNTRY FOR A YEAR, SO ANTICIPATING THE MOMENT
of reunion, my husband and I made a huge "welcome home, Lou" sign. I mentioned to a friend that the plan was to flash it high at the airport as he got off the plane, this piece of childish artwork with letters that had been filled in with a rainbow of magic-marker colors.

She rolled her eyes and remarked, "Are you sure when he sees it, he won't walk right past you?" I was sure. Even though he is a dignified 23, I knew he would love it.

It didn't quite work out according to plan. We got to the airport on time, but with the new airline quirk of landing 15 minutes ahead of schedule, he was hanging around wondering if anyone had thought to pick him up. He was headed for baggage claim when we ran into him.

We quickly unfurled our sign. He did love it. (So did a woman walking by who said, "Can I be Lou?")

It was a great reunion and treat to have him home after not seeing him for so long. He is fully a man now and a wonderful one at that. In the first few days, I found myself scrutinizing him, having this eerie thought: He is so clearly not of us any more. He is his own self-propelled entity.

Immediately he immersed himself in a job search, sending out resumes to Georgia, Colorado and Maine. Note I did not mention Cleveland, despite the allure of the Rock and Roll Hall of Fame and Museum and the Tribe's winning season.

I found myself wondering, what is it with this American rite of passage of having to move to some far-flung city? How did this get to be a measure of growing up? What happened to the days of tightknit families and tightknit neighborhoods, where, when a kid grew up, he moved into the house down the street. (Or was this a myth?)

The reunion turned out to be more ritual than reality.

In three short weeks, he had a job and was on his way again. It is not that I would have wished for him to stay. We get along well, but moving home would have crimped him.

And that's what growing up is all about, isn't it? Going off, becoming independent? So why was I unsettled?

It brought back my own "road not taken" at the same moment in my life. After I graduated from college, I boldly took a job in New Bedford, Mass. It was to begin in the fall. I came home to work for the summer. I would soon be off on some unknown adventure.

I never went. My summer employer offered me a permanent job, and my hometown became my home — a few miles from where I grew up — for almost 20 years. I was soon off on a different adventure — marriage and motherhood.

Over the years, I have often wondered, did I stay because it was a better job or because I needed to stick close to home?

You bring a child home all at once. But they leave by increments. My son's departure hit me again with the idea of home without children.

It also made me realize something else. As much as I have always thought I stood on my own feet, I saw how much my sense of self, my place in the world, was tied to having children. Not only the richness of it, but the sheer power that comes from it. How much they are an enhancer, a buffer, even a crutch. I felt bereft of it all.

So the homecoming was not a coming home. We will, of course, see him whenever we can. And we will, on some level, always be home. But home for him now is not so much a place as a yet unformed trajectory leading to what will someday be his own. ❧

49

the cleanser

EACH YEAR WHEN I WAS GROWING UP, MY MOTHER'S MOTHER, WHO LIVED IN CALIFORNIA, would come to visit us for a month in the summer. And each year, there would be great excitement anticipating her arrival.

We would shop for the foods she liked: prune juice, which she had every morning, chicken for roasting and extra milk, which she drank diluted with hot water before she went to bed. We'd get the guest room ready and remind each other of her quaint stories about the old country.

Things would go smoothly for a while. Then almost inevitably, they would break down. It would be over something like the kitchen cleanser. For my grandmother, the immutable place for the cleanser was on the top of the sink, right by the cold-water faucet. For my mother, who liked the counter clear, it was in the cabinet under the sink. As the days went on and they took turns cleaning the kitchen, the cleanser would go back and forth. Soon, if my mother was just passing by and found the cleanser on the sink, she would slam it underneath.

My grandmother, of course, was bewildered — why would anyone in her right mind keep the cleanser under the sink?

For me, it was a new and quite interesting view of my mother. She was a child again under the thumb of her mother. But later, as an adult, I developed a more sympathetic view. Her ways were never recognized by her own mother.

Unfortunately, the same became true for my siblings and me. My mother held onto the family that once was, even though after we moved into our own lives, that constellation no longer fit.

She and I lived in the same city, so our visits were never long enough under the same roof to tangle over the kitchen cleanser. But I never felt she saw me as I had become in my adult life. Our relationship consisted of returning to her context. My life, as I had made it for myself, was beyond her purview.

Now, I'm reaching this point with my own children. They are off at college. I am here with this empty nest. What a telling image of blankness, as if there is no script or even suggestion for how the relationship at this stage is to be. The popular sense is of this sad mother, apron strings dangling, and the bewildered father, hand empty now of ball in glove, going off into the golden sunset of old age.

It seems the end of the story. (Of course the nest is not really empty. The bills go on — tuition, long-distance phone calls, car insurance — into an indefinite future.)

Yet a visit a year ago to my older son at college struck me as something full of quite different possibilities. I spent a day with him, catching a glimpse of his adult shape — the warm, jaunty "What's up?" greeting to acquaintances on campus; the way he popped a tape in when he'd come into his room; his familiar high energy and intensity in action.

I was jolted into really seeing him, this person I had produced, free now to make his imprint — how, when or where he chooses. It was as if suddenly a new dimension was added to our relationship. This baby, child, teen, young man whom I had always seen from the inside out, I now saw from the outside in. It seemed a moment of official recognition of his privacy, his turf, his way of doing things.

So I say, hold the sunset. If life is long, this phase could go on twice as many years as childhood. And be just as rich, especially if we have half a chance to rise above the kitchen cleanser. ❧

c y c l i n g

MY SON MAX WENT THROUGH THE MOTIONS HIS SENIOR YEAR, TAKING THE SAT'S, FILLING out an application, sending in the deposit. But he did it begrudgingly and only after my constant reminding, cajoling and badgering.

He waited until a few days before freshman orientation and then he politely declined, saying no, thanks, he really couldn't do it. College, that is. He just didn't see himself sitting in class right now.

What he really wanted to do — in fact, planned to do — was what he loved: race his bicycle.

Cycling had been his obsession for three years and his emancipation. I often saw it as my nemesis.

In high school, he would train every day, even in winter. He would hit the road with his fellow racers, their taut, wiry bodies in skintight clothes, for six, eight, ten hours, whatever they could get in before dark, doing 60, 80, 100 miles.

I would ask, "Where are you going?"

He would answer with that adolescent precision, "I think southeast."

That might mean West Virginia. You don't know parental fear until you've seen an 18-wheeler on the highway pass your son on a bicycle, with its pencil-thin tires, or watched him go down with a pack of racers coming out of a tight turn.

He had his successes. His most thrilling was placing seventh in the junior nationals when he was 16. But so few achieve any consistent success in competitive cycling. And the defeats — the crashes, the flat tires 40 miles into a race or simply not being fit enough — are excruciating.

But none of this deterred him.

I can't say I was surprised at his announcement, which was a year-and-a-half ago. He never indicated he would follow a conventional path.

But I didn't take it well. That bike confounded me.

Education in my family is second only to breathing. The baby bottle is replaced with a book. I heard voices: The uncomprehending words of immigrant relatives, long gone, "What do you mean he wants to ride a bicycle?"

And the conclusions of the stacks of studies about the sorry future for kids with no college.

Other parents expressed admiration, outwardly at least. He was fit beyond what any of us could imagine. He had initiative, discipline, perseverance. And he was listening to his own drum.

As long as it wasn't their kid. I always felt an unspoken question: How do you allow this? And I always had an unspoken one of my own: How do you stop it?

High school had been in his way, and now it was behind him. He spent the year working at a bike shop, building bicycles and training every minute he could. Cycling seemed to have everything he wanted: camaraderie, competition, fitness, freedom, adventure. He was in a self-sufficient cocoon.

But it was tough going, saving enough money to get to races, then doing well once he got there. Ironically, I thought he was doing quite well. But it wasn't good enough for him.

At the end of the year, he announced he was quitting. The cocoon was giving way. He turned on a dime and put a toe in the waters of school; one course in the fall, two now. And he has even mentioned going full time. He left the bike shop for a job at a grocery store.

So when we talked the other day, he brought it up, and it wasn't the first time, that he was thinking of selling his bicycle. I was taken aback and suggested he not be too quick. Maybe he would want to take it up again.

No, he said he was pretty sure. He wanted to move on.

I suddenly felt a pang of nostalgia. But I said no more. One thing I know for sure: He'll decide. §

54

when the mind opens up

WAS IT NOT JUST YESTERDAY HE WAS GLIDING ALONG, DOING WHAT WAS EXPECTED? ALL OF A sudden in sixth, eighth, maybe ninth grade, something had changed, something imperceptibly had slipped away.

You know for sure now because you've seen a grade report, had a call from a teacher or two. Yes, all he or she is doing is going through the motions. At best erratic effort. Maybe not even that in math or English. More like disengagement.

You've been doing that "How's school?" "Fine" routine for weeks, trusting as we parents are wont to do, and all along he hasn't been doing a thing.

You watch closely. He seems to float as if none of it matters. Scattered papers, forgotten assignments, left books. The mind is simply elsewhere. Shut down, hibernating. You make pointed inquiries. You try to help. He looks you right in the face and says, "You know, school's not that interesting."

Imagine that. Only an oblivious, ignorant 14-year-old has the gall to dismiss hundreds of years of accumulated knowledge. So you whip out lecture No. 1: School is nothing less than the key to your future. And No. 2: Who gave you the right to check out of this? And No. 3: You don't have to like it, you just have to do it. In return you get those looks: glazed, angry, blank.

So you move on to the reprimands and groundings: no television, phone time, seeing friends until homework is done. Maybe tutoring or even a new school. You don't want to admit it, but one day you have to; this kid of yours, on the school front at least, is shut up like a clam. You try everything. But mostly you wait and wonder: Why did the mind shut down and when does it open up?

Other parents tell you about late bloomers. It is not that you don't see blossoming; it is just elsewhere. With music, friends, sports or partying. Mr. Too-Cool-for-School is in your house.

You look around for that chorus of other voices — a teacher, a counselor, aunt, grandfather, friend, brother. Where is that magic person who will get through?

The chorus tries, but no one makes a dent. What is going on inside him? You wish for some door to knock on. Hello, remember me? I'm on your side. Remember when you were once a cheerful, easygoing kid? Sorry, no one's home. Tuned out. He may stay that way for a long time.

Maybe he's not like a clam or a house with no door, but like an egg not ready to hatch. Because, as imperceptibly as when he fell away from books and learning, something changes again. One day he might say, "Do you know about… What do you think of…" The music is off. Conversation returns.

You can tell he feels an urgency to know more. He is becoming a learner not just in school, but in life. He is curious about the world — how it works and his place in it.

I don't know what, of all the things we parents do during these dark times, matters. Probably all of it. Perhaps some internal recording device has been on all this time, taking in all you've said. Nor do I know what teacher or book first penetrated his shell.

Maybe the mind, quite on its own, simply opened up. Suddenly, it is as if the gears click. All parts are in order and ready to do the work they were meant to do.

I have seen it, and I can tell you it's worth the wait. When the mind opens up, it is a beautiful thing. ৶

55

feeders and the fed

IT HAS OFTEN BEEN SAID THAT THE WORLD BREAKS DOWN INTO TWO KINDS OF PEOPLE. I COULDN'T agree more. To me, it is the feeders and the fed.

The fed live happy and spontaneous lives. They are utterly confident that, as hunger sends out its first faint twinge, meals will magically appear before them. They usually do. Not all, but most husbands and children fit into this category.

The feeders are in sharp contrast. Their lives are plodding and oppressed by responsibility. The subject of food rarely leaves their minds. They are always somewhere in the meal chain: planning, procuring, cooking, serving, eating or throwing away. Not all but many mothers fit into this category.

I'm one of them. I wonder, sometimes, if I would have lived my younger years differently had I known the amount of time I would spend keeping track of what several important people in my life put in their mouths in the course of a day. Was it prudent to spend so much time studying the Communist Revolution (now defunct) or principles of economics (long forgotten)?

The fed will poise themselves in front of an open refrigerator after the feeder has packed away eight bags of groceries and announce, "There's nothing to eat here!"

To them, what is on the refrigerator shelves is inert, unless it is leftover pizza. They don't do food preparation. The fed develop exotic food preferences — "I don't eat things mixed together" — that feeders are expected to honor.

The fed walk carefree out of the house, lunchbox swinging in hand, or off to a power lunch.

Feeders leave home bent over shopping lists, trying to figure out if they can get to the grocery store at lunchtime. Feeders feel obligated to finish what others leave on their plates. Feeders will eat anything and find it delicious, as long as someone else makes it.

I started becoming a feeder long ago, perhaps during pregnancy. Stretched before me was the seductive prospect of becoming Mother Earth. I bought the whole program: Feeding is part of the glue that holds a family together. Little did I know that I was creating an onerous class system that had me at the bottom.

Lovingly, I cleaned pureed peas out of babies' ears. In my mind's eye was the image of the serene family sitting down together passing bowls of homemade mashed potatoes to each other.

Not that it always worked that way. Family dining, at different stages, was laced with spilled food, outbursts of tears, kicks under the table, grievances, grunts, and resistance to helping.

I persevered. At my peak, by 8 a.m., I had already fed breakfast to two children, packed lunches for same, and, the biggie — decided what would be for dinner.

But before I knew it, this whole superwoman scenario was already unraveling. There's the competition. One night, soon after my oldest son started earning his own money on a paper route, he liberated himself: He called up and had a pizza delivered because he didn't like what we were having for dinner.

At a certain stage, the hamburger I made didn't compare to McDonald's or chicken to Kentucky Fried. I was still arguing that fast food had too much fat when one child got nutrition religion. Becoming practically vegetarian, suddenly my cooking came under fire as having too much fat.

Then children get busy with their own schedules. They eat their own meals at their own time.

In retrospect, it's a wonderful thing to see, the first baby steps to becoming a feeder, if only of themselves. And I, well, I have taken giant steps to joining the ranks of the fed. I accept all invitations. ✍

I AM SURE YOU KNOW HOW IT IS: YOUR FAMILY IS COMFORTABLE AT ONE STAGE; WHATEVER IS ahead is simply unimaginable. Your sweet, clean, cuddly baby will never be transformed into an uncouth 3-year-old who will declare war on you in the store because you won't buy Sugar Pops. Your cheerful 9-year-old, who collects comics and kisses you good-night, will never become a sullen teen whose stance is, "If you said it, it must be wrong."

But as surely as the planets revolve in their orbits, you will be there.

My family has entered another yet unimaginable stage. A few weeks ago, my younger child turned 21. There are no children any more. Actually, there haven't been for some time. Everyone is up on his own two feet. Everyone, for better or worse, is self-determining, if not fully self-supporting.

It coincided with a family gathering of my sisters, my husband's sister and their families, and so we made a grand party of it. I had a moment of panic, watching him blow out the candles. Where are we now, I wondered. Is this a family at all? Doesn't it defy at least one definition of family? Dependence. (I know what you are thinking, "Oh, these mothers, don't they ever let go?")

The operative word here was moment. Overall, I was mellow, sipping my wine. I settled into a not-altogether-unpleasant state. Actually, relief. "The job is done," I thought. This birthday crosses the T's, dots the I's.

These days, of course, 18 is the age of emancipation, when you leave home and can vote, be tried as an adult and be drafted if there was a war. I see 18 to 21 as an in-between time. The bird is definitely out of the nest. But the parental wing is still flapping, even if it flaps mostly for itself. Worry is still on active duty.

At 21, the line between us is firm. His worries are his own. It is up to him to make sense of his life. I actually felt a sigh of relief. I was no longer responsible.

This was not empty nest, mind you. I have been there, getting snagged at unexpected moments on some wisp of nostalgia, such as the absence of stuff cluttering the kitchen or other people's children walking home from school.

No, this was that unimaginable stage out beyond the horizon of empty nest. It was time to pack up those overdeveloped and, of late, underutilized tools of motherhood. It was time to lay down my stringent expectations of myself to be the good mother. What is done is done.

Of course, I would always be there for both of my sons if they were feeling blue, wanted to talk through a tough decision, were in trouble or ill. It is also likely that if I was facing some difficult event, these now twentysomething sons would come through for me.

We are still connected by powerful bonds. The telephone relationship, in fact, is in its full ascendancy. After news and plans for this and that, the question — "And how are you?" — has begun to emerge from the other end of the line. We seem to have entered something approaching mutuality.

Like planets moving in their orbits, we are lined up in a new way. I never imagined this bonus, when family is not predicated on dependence of either generation, when we are all in it by choice for the sheer pleasure of each other.

I was, for a moment, reminded of my mother saying, "I never want to be dependent on you kids." Then one day she was. My husband and I will enjoy these harvest years for as long as they last until the next, as yet unimaginable, stage. ❧

APRIL 26TH IS IT. MY SECOND SON, MAX, IS GRADUATING FROM COLLEGE. WE ARE NOT BIG ON formalities, and he will be one among thousands at this huge university. But I believe life offers few enough honors, so we should soak up the sunshine. Graduating from college is one of them. My husband and I will be there. Especially for this son. He did it his way, every step of it, sometimes the hard way.

He began six years ago, a part-time, night-school student not even sure he wanted to be there. He will graduate with distinction from the honors college with a passion for his subject — history — and then on, he hopes, to graduate school. I am grateful to this school that took him where he was and never stopped challenging him to do more.

The university did its job. But Max did much more. There is no degree or honor for growing up, something offspring must do quite on their own. They must somehow sort out the tangles we lay upon them and those they lay upon themselves. It takes a certain grit.

Max's path has been an unconventional one, quite different from his older brother's. We moved to Cleveland his junior year of high school, and he did not take root. The next year we reluctantly agreed he could go back to Pittsburgh, live with friends of ours and finish at his old school. I was bereft and felt we left him stranded at a time when he was most in need. But perhaps his need was not for us.

It took a certain pluck not to go to college in this family that puts a high value on academics. But he declined. His dream was to be a long-distance bicycle racer. He went for it and with some success. A year later he enrolled in school. He dyed his hair a crazy orange. All the while he supported himself working long hours at a pizza shop among a narrow-minded, mean-spirited group of co-workers. He began to learn something of what he was not.

It was when he took his first history class that he began to get grounded in who he was — first by studying the history of his people. Then he plunged into a broader world of conflict and struggle. He had found his metier.

You might say we left home, he didn't. He has re-created a life for himself where he grew up. He lives in the same old city neighborhood where we, my parents and their parents once lived. Now, walking around, it is he who waves to the young people who inhabit this area.

We love his apartment, a decent one, finally. We keep threatening to vacation there. It is my hometown too, my roots after all. Cozy with big windows and good heat, it is in an old, funky building, populated with the elderly, students and new immigrants.

About a year ago, I made a new display of family photos as parents do when their children have left home. Many of our pictures are of our two sons together, a pair, even twinned, as they were in some ways when they were young. They are only 19 months apart, for me practically an unbroken experience of baby.

The new display of photos pictures them separately. And the photos of each are clustered in different spaces as they, in fact, now are.

Max's hair is a natural brown again, a conservative cut. He rolls his eyes when he is reminded of that time when he spent hours on a bicycle. What a waste, all those miles of hard pedaling, he will say. But I see he took something with him — a certain grit, perseverance to get his focus and his life right.

This is new terrain for me. My father died when I was 23. My mother kind of resigned from parenthood after that. From then on, I was to be there for her to depend on. So there is this unexpected pleasure of sharing interests, ideas and events in frequent and free wheeling conversations, barely tinged with the parental.

But there is still one event where I intend to feel like a mom. Graduation. April 26. I'll be there. ❧

61

a n n i v e r s a r y

I'M FEELING LIKE A BIT OF AN ODDITY THESE DAYS. IN TWO WEEKS MY HUSBAND, DAVID, AND I will mark 25 years of marriage.

Divorce is so commonplace, we're practically an endangered species.

We have never been big on ritual. We didn't have much of a wedding — a simple ceremony and lunch with our families. Sometimes at a big wedding, my heart will quicken with the music, the white dress. But I have no regrets. I didn't want to be on display and I was wary of the whole "bride" schtick. It felt like the start of getting slotted into a female role I was going to find confining.

Apparently, I didn't find it so. It staggers me that I have been married 25 years. It makes even me wonder what the secret is to a lasting marriage, as the women's magazines say. For one, I was never big on the "losing myself" kind of love, the oneness, the merging kind of relationship. I think of simply David and me.

For another, I don't think of "the marriage" as a distinct entity. Just the sound of the phrase "institution of marriage" makes me feel there is no room to breathe or grow. Again, I think more of simply David and me.

Once, I heard someone say the first 20 years of marriage are rough. After that it gets easier. It was supposed to be a joke, but there's some truth to it. In recent years, we have reached a plateau. There's a lot we don't have to hash out with each other any more. We know where the other is, and we are willing to grant room to be there. It may be love and passion that bind us together, but oh, how long it takes to be truly aware of the other person.

There are ways in which we are profoundly different. David is reserved and decisive. I talk things through, in his view, maddeningly. He is tidy. I am, shall I say, less so.

He is far more forceful than I. He can take a stand in the face of opposition, rescue a person in an emergency. He is a fighter, a survivor. He can get rid of a mouse on the back step. It leaves me in awe.

Still, our values are a near mirror-image of each other. The way he thinks, reacts and sees the world is as interesting to me today as it was when I first became intrigued with him. He is my best friend.

When I wake in the middle of the night in a cold sweat because I don't have a column idea, he offers worthy suggestions. He has also gone along with my writing about him. What trust.

Finally, it seems, we have each come around to conceding a few faults. I have made some unilateral decisions. I don't take proper care of my car. I harbor grievances. Yes, they are quite vivid.

There is his excess of magazine subscriptions, his hankering for a Harley, his knack for rewriting history to put a positive spin on, I guess you could say, my grievances.

Still that old cliché of lasting marriage — compromise — is true. And I don't mean the little stuff, like, OK, we'll go to the movie you want. I mean in substantial ways, like we are in this together and there are no guarantees.

When all is said and done, it comes down to this: We get along. With David, I can be myself. I think he feels the same way. That is no small thing.

When our son Max was a baby, he had his special blankie from which he would not be separated. It was worn and unraveling. Eight years ago, when I was facing surgery and cancer treatments and bemoaning the body mutilation ahead, David said to me, "It doesn't matter. I will still love you even if you get as tattered as Max's blankie." I will never forget it.

And so, it is unlikely we will get involved in any fanfare. Maybe dinner out and a movie. Still, 25 years is worth noting. ❧

63

the guitar

THE HOUSE IS QUIET, BUT NO LONGER IS IT THE EMPTY SILENCE OF CHILDREN WHO HAVE RECENTLY departed for their own lives. It is a richer solitude perhaps because at odd moments here and there the house is filled with music. With increasing frequency, my husband, David, picks up his guitar — after work, on a Sunday afternoon, at night when we get home from somewhere. Suddenly he is singing again, old favorites or new — an Eric Clapton song, Alison Krauss or the Eagles, "Love Will Keep You Alive."

Whenever he plays, I find myself stopping what I am doing. Sometimes I stand by the door of the room where he is playing, listening, not wanting to interrupt.

In the glow of the desk light in the corner, he will be sitting sideways on the edge of the chair, his foot tapping — always keeping time — one hand picking and strumming, the other pressing the chords. His soft, clear tenor voice, enveloped in the rich sound of the 12-string guitar, washes over me.

When we met, he was in the midst of turning a corner into a new life. He had been making his living as a musician. He was part of a popular local folk music trio, two men and a woman, two guitars and a banjo. Suddenly he was putting a suit on every day.

The group was breaking up, going straight you might say, getting real jobs. For a while, anyway, the old life hung on. They kept playing Saturday nights at the same funky bar they had played at for years. They performed on a small platform in a spot of light behind the bartender. It was an intimate little place — dark, smoke-filled and overheated with wall-to-wall people.

They had a regular following of fans to banter with, who called out requests. I was too naive, too square, too much on the fringe to even be a groupie. But that soft tenor voice singing those mournful ballads of love and loneliness… Well, I was smitten.

It was not long before his music was submerged by his new career and the cacophony of family life. As kids have a way of doing, ours laid our every foible bare. We saw each other at the worst and through the worst.

Now it seems we have rounded that corner, as parents eventually do, out of the dark side of adolescence. We find ourselves blinking in the sun. A quiet has come over us, a hard-won privacy. I am amazed to find we are intact and still, in our own ways, moved by the same pleasures. Like the sound of the guitar.

Of course it has taken some reclamation. Years ago, David gave the guitar he had used for years to one of his singing partners. Then, one day not long ago, on impulse, he bought a beautiful new one for himself.

Then he staked out a room of his own. Our second floor has been in a state of flux as grown children come and go. This room was rarely used by one of our sons, other than as a repository for stuff. David put in a table to use for his desk. The guitar stands in the corner.

So at these odd moments, he plays. I listen to him picking out the chords and getting down the words to a whole new batch of songs. I see him sitting on the edge of the chair, tapping his foot, strumming.

He is an older man now, with glasses and hair graying at the temples. But he is also as I first remember him, his soft, clear tenor voice enveloped in the rich sounds of the guitar.

I stand by the door letting the music wash over me. It fills the quiet of the house. ❧

arthur in pittsburgh

AS WE OFTEN DO, MY HUSBAND AND I MADE THE 2½-HOUR TRIP EAST A FEW WEEKS AGO TO visit my father-in-law. We came laden with offerings: He, a new reading lamp; I, two bags of groceries. Actually, a meal — meatloaf, scalloped potatoes, salad, dressing, homemade bean soup, bread and an apple pie.

Arthur, as I call him, will turn 90 this year. He has lived on his own since my mother-in-law died 13 years ago. We try to care for him, but it's not easy. Unless something is done his way, he rejects it. His world has declined since we moved a few years ago.

First, he refused a volunteer program that would help with the things I had done: groceries, laundry, trips to the doctor. "Why, they wanted my Social Security number," he told me indignantly.

Then I tried a grocery store that delivered. Out of the question. "Did you see the prices they charged?" he accused.

Only gradually, begrudgingly, has he let the volunteers into his life. We no longer discuss his moving to a place where he could get more help. Last year, my husband drove in to take him to visit one. Arthur had changed his mind and wouldn't go.

He spent his career as a book buyer for department stores. When we lived in the same city, people would ask me in awe if I was related to the man who expounded on literary themes and criticism.

He spends his days reading. Every wall of his modest home is lined with books of the great writers and philosophers. He has read all of them, many more than once.

He walks with a cane because his knees are weak with arthritis. He is bent over and his speech is halting. He fears falling, especially if it might mean a trip to the hospital.

My husband sets up the lamp. I unpack the food. He rejects only the salad dressing. "Too spicy," he said, handing it back. I think of my effort as successful.

The refrigerator has only milk, a few eggs, two oranges. The cupboard where dishes once were holds the provisions of his spare existence: Quaker Oat Squares, dry-roasted peanuts, cans of Chunky Clam Chowder, a stack of chocolate bars. On the kitchen table are a single dish and cup. Pantry shelves are stacked with books.

We sit. He talks, a melange of world events, big ideas and the themes of Melville. My husband has heard these recitations all his life. Only recently has he developed patience for them.

I have heard them since our children were young, when Arthur, recently retired, would help me take them to the playground. He would talk of Phillip Roth as I caught children at the bottom of the slide and wiped runny noses. He brought welcome discourse into my days of three-word sentences. And he would spend hours reading to them and my husband's oldest son, Jonathan.

As Arthur talked that day, my eye took in his unique home decorating. Place mats were on upholstered chairs where doilies used to be. The bathtub mat was by the front door. Few vestiges were left of the cozy home my mother-in-law had made.

So I arrive again in my mind at our dilemma. Arthur does not live well. Sometimes he seems like a child, poorly fed and clothed, on the loose in the neighborhood. Yet he has what matters to him: his home, his books and the fierce fantasy that he takes care of himself, even though most days it's Chunky soup and chocolate bars.

So, I'm planning ham, green beans, macaroni and cheese for my husband to take when he returns next week. And he has bought an extension cord for the lamp. &

a r t h u r   w i t h   u s

MY FATHER-IN-LAW, ARTHUR, TURNED 90 LAST YEAR, AND IT SEEMS LIFE'S STRUGGLE HAS NOT LESSENED. In fact, the issue of recent years — dignity — is, if anything, more pressing.

I'm mostly an observer. My husband, David, now for the first time, is front and center, the nurturer. But I'm glad to be along. My own father died within a week of his 53rd birthday. Arthur has now been in my life as long as my own father was.

Arthur has lived alone in a nearby city since his wife died 14 years ago. But in recent years, as arthritis and a pervasive frailty settled in, it has become increasingly difficult for him to get around. Neighbors have helped with shopping and other errands, but his world has gotten smaller. It has become confined mostly to the first floor of his house. The steps, up to the bathroom and down to get outside, have become almost insurmountable.

Everything, down to the smallest logistic, is a struggle: cutting food, getting his belt in the loops, placing his hands precisely in the right place on the chair arms in order to push himself up. A walker is now integral to standing, balancing, walking and his sense of well-being.

After emergency surgery last summer, he told us he wanted to move here, so we found him a place for assisted living. With his fierce independence, it was a heroic decision, a begrudging concession to reality. He has a deep dread of hospitals and a loathing for nursing homes, which he calls "nursery care." He finds any form of institutional behavior insulting.

So we had some trepidation about his reaction to his new home. "Why, it's a medical hotel" was his outraged first impression. But with his usual grit, he set about re-creating his life.

Much about it is better. He gets nutritious hot meals in a dining room with tablecloths, help with a bath, his laundry done. And he can get outside.

But the transition was hard. At first I think he found it both astonishing and depressing to look around and see that he was now living in a place where everyone was quite old.

And he lost a lot: being part of a real neighborhood, a breeze blowing through the living room in the summer, children visiting and leaving their scratchy drawings, a mailman who came to the door, neighbors who were young and worked at jobs and laughed and planned a garden in the common back yard.

The real plus is for the father and the son, now finally in some alignment with one another. David visits almost every day. When he arrives, Arthur becomes warm and animated. David sets about shaving him, making sure his sweets drawer is stocked and solving the issues of the day.

That might be getting him shoes he can get on himself or a jacket closing changed to Velcro because the zipper is too difficult. Being independent comes down to just these kinds of mechanics.

Arthur's passion has always been books. He spent his career as a book buyer for department stores. On a much smaller scale now, he has re-created this world. His chair is next to a bookshelf where he arranges the books he is currently interested in.

The big, big loss is in the eyes. He has great difficulty reading. So David, and a few others where he lives, reads to him.

He has settled in, doing again what he has always done, turning over in his mind the mysteries of the printed word. When I go to visit, I too listen to David read. And I am enlightened, as I always have been, by some unique thought Arthur has to share. ❧

l o s i n g   a r t h u r

THE NURSING HOME CALLED ONE SATURDAY MORNING LAST MONTH. MY FATHER-IN-LAW WAS quite ill. When my husband and I got there, the staccato movements of nurses fluttered around him. Arthur was in a helpless agony.

The son held onto his father's hand, and they looked into each other's eyes much as we do when we are first on this earth. Soon the morphine took over and he was peaceful. In a few hours, he died. The movie "Apollo 13" blared outside his room where most of the other residents, poised in front of it, dozed.

You think you are ready, more than ready. He was 93. He talked of life being a burden to him. He told many he was ready to die. Several ailments had converged in a downward spiral with no prospect of reversal. There were to be no more hospitalizations. Still, the imprint of his fear, his pain that day will not fade easily from my mind.

Even when life has been very long, when death happens, it lands with the same thud, leaving the same shock and numbness. A few weeks later we gathered, past the immediate grief of first knowing.

They came from Miami and New Mexico, Chicago, New York and Pittsburgh, children and grandchildren, a niece and great nephew. My husband's aunts from the other side of the family came. So did the remnant of Arthur's friends, as well as a few of mine who cooked and baked and brought big bowls of food and tins of pastries.

It was hard to know how to honor this formidable patriarch who had no ritual in his life. My husband called the event part Quaker, part Irish, part Jewish.

First we sat in a large group and those who wished shared their stories or thoughts of him. Some were admiring, some funny, some sad.

When the son's voice faltered, his own son touched his knee.

There were other breaking voices, including my own. I talked of what it was like to be welcomed into the protective fold of this family, of what a cushion they were for me when my children were young.

Arthur and I were kind of thrown together. About the time he retired, I left full-time work to care for children. So we were both desperate for a little company. He would walk over and help me take the kids to the park or read or build with them.

His world was books so we would talk of Dostoevsky or Fitzgerald as I changed diapers. It was welcomed discourse. Later, I believe, it was experiencing his infatuation with the written word that led me to writing.

The talk was not all glowing. It was said more than once that he was a difficult man. Yet we had stuck with him. As I looked around, I could not help feeling that the fact of our gathering was a triumph.

Then we drank and talked and renewed connections: "Come to Chicago." "We will!" And, of course, we ate heartily, ending fittingly with a joyous birthday celebration for one of the grandsons.

Sometime in that day of reunion and communal grieving, in that public acknowledgment of loss, was a closure. I could almost feel the family constellation move down a generation.

The private grief, of course, goes on. Each death, I have found, has a way of reopening all the deaths that have dotted my life.

Recently, while my husband and I were sitting in a restaurant, a family seated themselves next to us. We both fixed on the elderly father with those familiar wisps of white hair. We watched the efforts of the grown son as he eased his father into his chair. A simple, caring gesture. Our lives were once filled with thousands of them, loving and obligatory. No more.

The last parent is gone. No one is ahead of us now. No matter how frail the older generation becomes, it is still protective. Suddenly the loss felt like the absence of a woolen sweater on a cold March day. ᕽ

a u n t   i z z i e

A WEEK OR SO AGO, I WENT TO MY HOMETOWN TO VISIT MY AUNT ISABELLE. IN RECENT YEARS SHE has spent all of her time caring for her ill husband. Then a few months ago, she was hit with two blows. She needed heart bypass surgery. Just after she arrived home from the hospital to begin her recovery, her husband, Joe, my mother's brother, died. Aunt Isabelle was not even well enough to go to his funeral.

I had some trepidation about seeing this stalwart aunt in what I imagined to be a debilitated state. Afflictions of the heart seem to plague my family. My mother died three months after heart surgery. Images of her fragility crept into my mind.

Aunt Isabelle is near 80 now. Her hair, always short and curled around her face, is grayer. She is thinner, smaller. But when I saw her coming out of her apartment building to meet me, all these signs of aging were incidental. I felt an instant rush of relief and pleasure. She reached out, and her familiar sparkle leaped up to me from her pale blue eyes and sweet smile. She was still my Aunt Izzie, or Iz, as my sisters, brother and I had always called her.

We went to a neighborhood restaurant for dinner. There she recounted her ordeal. She still has difficulty breathing and pain in her chest from the healing. She showed me the incision in her leg where the veins were taken to be used in the bypass. I was awed by her acceptance, her coexistence with pain, illness and loss.

She spoke of being alone, how small her world had become in the years of caring for her husband. We recounted the family members who had died. She listed friends who were gone or ill.

Yet she is sending out a few tendrils. The week before my visit, she had gone to the movies with two women in her building. She has other dinner invitations. She's thinking of going back to volunteer work.

"I go out," she said. "But when I go back into the apartment, I burst into tears." The absence of her husband of 54 years was like an amputation.

For the first time, I felt a glimmer of the meaning of the word survival.

I went back to her apartment for a while to help stave off her loneliness. She pulled out pictures of children and grandchildren. I have not seen them in so long that for a moment I mistake her grandson for my cousin when he was a kid.

Aunt Izzie and Uncle Joe once ran a jewelry and gift store in a dying mill town. They took it over from his parents — my grandparents — who started it in the boom days of steel. It was only because of Aunt Izzie's resoluteness that they managed to eke out a living. Their lives were a struggle. Ours were not.

Still, in my mind, Aunt Izzie had something of the ideal about her. She was the one who produced the luscious blueberry pies with crisscross crusts on family occasions. Compared to my mother, she seemed a sanctuary of reason. Or perhaps she became an alternative to me because my mother once told us that if ever anything happened to her, Aunt Izzie would care for us.

I mentioned to her this place she had in my life. She brushed it aside with a laugh. "All mothers not your own look better."

A humble nod to aunthood, to its great potential to fill the crevices mothers cannot reach.

Suddenly, I was aware that Aunt Izzie is my last connection to my parents' generation. My mother and father and all their siblings are gone now. And so I was glad to be touched once again by this special aunt, this smidgen of family still left. ❧

73

74

t w o   s o n s

I AM WALKING ALONG THE STREET, ABOUT 20 FEET BEHIND MY TWO SONS. THEY ARE TALKING TO each other, one explaining and gesticulating, the other listening, then back and forth again.

I am having trouble keeping up. Perhaps it is because these young men — 24 and 23 — have such long strides. For the past six months, my older son, Lou, has been working in a foreign land. My husband and I and our younger son, Max, are visiting for two weeks. It has been a long time since the four of us have spent this much time together.

There is some advantage to falling behind. I can watch them. I am, in fact, mesmerized. I am struck by how large they are, how much space they take up walking down the street. And I am struck by their vastly different forms, now fully realized.

Lou is broad-chested, with long muscular arms, compact and powerful both naturally and from his years of athletic training. His hair is close-cropped, adding to his serious, intense look. Wearing a T-shirt, vest and hiking boots, he has a casual style.

Max is taller and has a long and slender body. His short, brown, curly hair frames his face. He dresses stylishly and teases his older brother about his tattered look.

Watching their easy conversation, I can't help but recall their differences: Lou's strength, both of body and will; Max's humor and easy social manner. Once these were the ways they battled each other.

Now they simply are. Each has such a different presence, I wonder now how we ever managed to wrap around them and blend as a family.

They are both past the sullen moods, the high-pitched battles of adolescence. Even their hair, which at one time for one or the other of them was shaved, dyed or grown long, seems to have diminished as a mode of self-expression.

Not that they don't have their "issues," as the expression goes. They do. You know as a parent that you do hundreds, no thousands, of things well — or at least adequately. Still, it's uncanny how offspring have this radar to zero in on what you might have missed or where you fell down.

So we take in sights, travel, talk and eat together. I listen to my older son order from the menu, argue with a taxi driver, joke with a friend in a foreign tongue. I am in awe, but seeing him so far into another culture gives me a strange distant feeling just as when he first insistently pushed off my lap after a feeding and crawled across the floor.

I listen to them reminisce. "Remember the time you beat up James Walsh?" Max asks. A legendary story, apparently, of which I have only the vaguest recollection.

And the thrilling game of cops and robbers with Nicky, William and Luciano on bicycles in the alleys and one-way streets of our old neighborhood. "Remember racing down that hill and through the intersection?"

I wonder, where exactly was I? Probably making dinner, believing they were innocently riding bikes and asking when they got home, "How was it?"

"Fine," they would say, happy and tired. I was outside of their lives even then, blissfully ignorant of these memorable games.

We came together, but it was different from our old configuration. Something is dissolved. It is that right — and responsibility — to imprint. That claim: They are mine! No more.

Sure, I can, with either son, discuss, ponder, question, suggest, commiserate, rejoice and empathize.

But what was perfectly clear as I watched them walk together along that street in front of me was that they have fully claimed their lives. ☙

passion for parenting

AT ONE TIME, I HAD ALL THE ANSWERS. BEING A PARENT WAS MY SERIOUS ENDEAVOR, AND I was forever giving serious consideration to the matter at hand, arriving at the "right" way, or at least my way of doing things.

Was it better to breast-feed or use a bottle? A pacifier or no? Pick the baby up when he cries or let him cry it out?

Each in turn was the great question of the day. Allow playing with toy guns, plastic swords? Spank or "time-out"? A definite bedtime? A homework time? Public school or private? Candy or no? And how much television? Get up from the table before everything on the plate is finished?

It is the passion of a new parent to engage these questions. And of course, you're always new, always on the cusp. The first child keeps getting older and changing. As soon as you get one stage down, he's on to the new one, and it's all puzzling and out of sync again. The next child is so radically different. Nothing is the same as it was with the first, and so on.

It is a kaleidoscopic universe. At the same time, as a family you reach for certitudes. This is who we are, this is how we do things, this is what we stand for. These answers are formed in the thousand decisions, large and small, you make about child-rearing.

Perhaps, too, this need to invent the rules is more pronounced in American child-rearing. We aren't willing to take as truisms what our parents did. We want to start clean or at least make improvements on the previous model.

So we listen to the parenting experts, read the how-to books, debate these questions with friends. It can lead one to the sense that child-rearing is amenable to reason, that cause and effect are strongly at work here.

But I now have doubts. I still have that new-parent passion. The new, however, is that my children are grown and have left home, leaving me less sure of the answers than I have ever been. I find myself wondering what all the intensity and immense energy was about. How does it all add up?

The years of raising children seem to telescope. The whole business of child-rearing seems much more mysterious. I am far less clear on what produces what result.

How children actually turn out is perplexing. The difficulties you may see in a child, say one who is stubborn and headstrong, may actually turn out to be strengths once he is out in the world. Something that was once a constant worry may simply evaporate. Or a child may take in what you least intended, such as your fears or insecurities. Only later does it become clear that children themselves, for better or worse, bring a great deal to the whole business of growing up.

Sure there are tangible things you can point to. I taught them to swim. But all that now seems like the busy work of parenting. Who you are, deep within your character, has at least as much influence as anything you do.

What's more, all those good decisions do not protect your children. The best you can hope for is that they are able to get on with their lives. Like the rest of us, they will have their own share of worries and anxieties to wrestle with.

I don't mean to imply that what you do doesn't matter. Of course it all matters. But from this vantage point, there's much more latitude than I ever thought.

So I'm coming around to a different emphasis. It is not so much having all the answers, but the passion you bring to the whole endeavor. That's what sticks. That's what makes you the parent of your particular child. Many answers work, but it is your passion that endures. ⸱

g r o w i n g   u p

WHEN MY CHILDREN WERE IN MIDDLE SCHOOL, I WENT TO A LECTURE AT ONE OF THOSE OPENING-of-school-year events that for some reason has always stuck in my mind.

It was a talk by a prominent psychiatrist titled something like," What to Expect in Your Middle School Child."

I went with great anticipation. Here I was with children in sixth and seventh grades, on the cusp of what a chorus of voices had warned would be the dark, tumultuous years.

My fantasy was that I would find the wisdom that would unlock the keys to adolescence. I wanted this speaker, world-weary from seeing too many dysfunctional families, to tell me what to do to avoid the scourges of drugs and alcohol, depression and getting derailed from school. I wanted no less than the secret elixir that would give my children safe passage.

Today, I cannot help but see the hubris in such a wish. Somehow my children would avoid the pain and pitfalls of growing up. It was also the hubris of young parents who believe they begin this endeavor of parenting with a clean slate. When the humbling truth is that we carry the imprint of generations.

Actually, I don't remember much of what this speaker said other than his finale, which is the part that has stayed with me: The best thing you can do as parent, he said, is take care of yourself.

What a statement. What a curveball. Now that was not the advice I was looking for. Here I was busy with the daily work of parenting: homework to stay on top of, getting them to activities and friends, dentist appointments and new shoes.

I wanted answers. At that stage you believe parenting is about what you do, which, of course, a great deal of it is. Only later do you find out how much of it is about, deeper down, who you are.

What I have come to understand about what this speaker meant is that becoming a better parent sometimes means tending to matters in your own life — for example, your relationship with your own parents and siblings. Or whether you can say what you mean when you are angry without either exploding or feeling too stifled. It would be nice if we could shape and influence our children only in the ways we want to. But no, they get the whole package, they get all of who we are.

Perhaps what he said stuck in my mind because it has taken me a long time to grow into it. I know now that one of the best things you do for your children is tend to the struggles in your own life. Now that my children are adults, I have a much longer vantage, so I would even add something to that talk I heard many years ago.

Let it be your hope that you manage to grow up before your children do.

Now that statement may perplex you. I don' t mean the tangible things of growing up like getting tall or shaving or wearing lipstick. Of course, in those things you are obviously ahead of your children.

What I am talking about is something else. You can teach a child to ride a bike and not to steal. You can enforce a curfew. But the time will inevitably come when they reach for the real you. What will they find?

A parent who could not control his or her temper? Or one who works all the time, avoiding the intimacy of family. A parent who could not take on responsibility? Or one who could not stand up for himself? Or a parent who could not listen to another point of view? Or one with unexamined prejudices or unacknowledged addictions?

Or will they find a powerful role model: A parent who has struggled to overcome whatever the difficulties may be.

If you want a relationship with your offspring that goes on when they are adults, the best thing you can do is the hard work of tending to yourself. And indeed, hope that you grow up before your children do. ❦